Prosperity Affirmations

In the
mountain
presence...
Great Gratitude

for all students, clients and colleagues...
who have given life to these prospering words
and most, to michael who gives
pages, bindings and typeset to all
our books of good thought.

may all who use these affirmations
rise above vocabularies born-into
and create vast futures unlike the past
to dance into.... with plenty to spare + share.

♡ toni Stone
June 13, 2002
fairfax, Vermont

Wonder Works Studio
401 Buck Hollow Road
Fairfax, VT 05454

Copyright© 2007 by Toni Stone

Cover photography by
Marie Ryan Pappas, e-mail: feb2639@webtv.net

Produced in the United States of America
by **Color PrePress Consulting**, Williston, Vermont

ISBN 0-942953-09-6

Toni Stone's
Prosperity Affirmations
Table of Contents

Table of Contents - con't

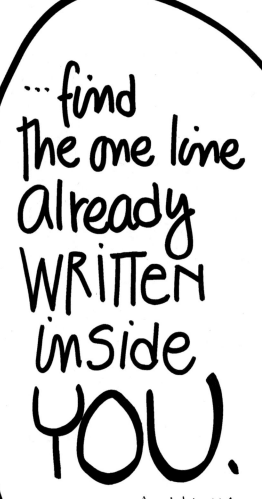

...find the one line already written inside you.

-david WHYTE
THE HOUSE OF BELONGING 1999

april 2002

in the design of

all There IS

everything moves in right relationship

i am part of That

Movement

perfect, whole and complete
i welcome The change of seasons and all that
That brings to me.

change is The law of life...
i welcome CHANGE.

i am willing to observe what changing would
empower me to be, do and have more POSSIBILITY.
i change words, thoughts, habits and patterns.
moving from The OLD to The NEW with ease and joy
i am grateful to feel free
TODAY
i am Happy

all is well in my WORLD.

i recognize
and release resistance to changing

❖ i realize that always to do things
   the way i've done them is to stay the same.
❖ i have the idea of changing...
   i'm willing to start changing.
❖ i am able to have and receive NEW DIRECTIONS.
❖ fully aware and fully awake, i am willing to prosper.
   i disassemble structures that insure stagnation.
❖ i am living immediately without previous limits...
   no limits allowed, no limits exist!
❖ no longer am i hesitant taking on risk...
   i recognize stops, they disappear.
❖ i invent and approve new experiences
   that evolve me to higher states.
❖ my vision reveals WHAT'S NEXT FOR ME... i am exuberant.
❖ i complete what's been, and move to what's not yet been...
❖ resistance dissolved.... ENTHUSIASM has replaced it...
❖ endings create new beginnings, forward into the process.
❖ i am ready to receive NEXT DIRECTIONS.
❖ new directions, create new ideas as seeds for starting.
❖ processing for what's new has already begun.
❖ i retain full assurance
   in all that's falling apart...new seeds emerge.
❖ letting go of what's been, is good now, i can be sure.
❖ i move into PROSPERITY CONSCIOUSNESS now.

give up being afraid and conflicted

❖ seeing what's possible replaces all conflicts certainly.
❖ today we have recognition of peace in our experience.
❖ we give up being afraid and conflicted, in the face of change.
❖ confused thoughts about changing are healed and given up...
❖ patterns we no longer wish to use
            now fall by the wayside...
            We are renewed by all manner of changes today.

relinquishment

❖ i relax and relinquish confusion. i choose to be happy now.
❖ i do not have to know "why" about one thing...
❖ i give up hidden scripts that hinder....
❖ my innocence is already established.
❖ i give up complaining, judging and assessing everything.
❖ i do not defend myself or explain anything else.
❖ i give up happiness-preventing scripts from past history.

❖ i do not have to find or search for anything more, i am happy.

prosperity attitudes

❖ i start now, wherever i am, i am acting in PROSPEROUS WAYS.

❖ i appreciate and use abundantly the money i have right now.

❖ both my hands are open, to give as well as receive.

❖ i give freely now.

❖ FINANCIAL TRANSACTIONS start with ME.

❖ i make VOLUNTARY OFFERINGS on a regular basis.

❖ giving is becoming a way of life for me.

❖ i give in small ways all the time, i tip extra, i pay a little more than my regular fare; i welcome the chance to throw in the extra something. this context opens me up to a LARGER CONTEXT of giving.

❖ i know that MY supply increases through sharing, I SHARE THE THING I WANT MOST TO GET.

❖ i know the universe will do for me what i am actively doing for it...as i give, it is given to me.

❖ my attitude towards life is MY choice, i CHOOSE an attitude of ABUNDANCE.

❖ the act of giving is freeing to my mind.

❖ generously i give and richly i receive...

❖ i have a SYSTEMATIC GIVING; a percentage of what i get goes back out in a voluntary fashion.

❖ i keep in touch with ideas, things and people that help me keep my PROSPERITY attitudes.

❖ i leave behind a feeling of being separated from wealth.

❖ i leave behind an attitude of lack.

❖ it is easier and easier for me to GIVE AWAY MONEY.

❖ giving enlivens and empowers me.

❖ now that i ENJOY GIVING, people love giving to me.

❖ i always have what's wanted and needed and more to give away... there is plenty. i know it.

prosperous thinking

✤ i know i cause the way i look at things.
✤ i break through barriers and limitations.
✤ i am responsible for what is in my mind.
✤ i am responsible for all my feelings.
✤ i am moving from scarcity to abundance.

✤ i am moving away from holding back
   and moving toward pressing out expressing myself.
✤ money has been for survival
   ...money is now a way i am enabled to express myself.
✤ money has been what i try to get
   ...money is now what i always have.
✤ i shift the way i have held ideas of money.
✤ i choose new ideas about money.
✤ i joyously move from scarcity to abundance...i have
   consciousness of plenty.
✤ i am willing to leave behind all limits and venture forth.
✤ i leave behind unconsciousness in financial matters.
✤ i move into being responsible for my forward movement.
✤ i experience my self as cause of how it is for me.
✤ i am responsible for what's in my mind.
✤ thinking creates results, i think about what i intend.

prosperous declarations

❖ i grow in prosperity, wisdom and understanding.

❖ i say yes to prospering now .

❖ prosperity is my native, natural condition.

❖ EXCELLENT CHOICES are now being made.

❖ good is always at work with me.

❖ good is constantly in mind,
  body and circumstances... as i prosper.

❖ wise abundance now surrounds me.

❖ i am CUT FREE from all former economic limitation.

❖ ABUNDANCE is now outpoured.
  OPULENCE is the natural state of life.

❖ all humankind shall express prosperity.

❖ this world is alive with Divine prospering.

❖ GOD IS THE SOURCE OF ALL MY GOOD.

❖ these words of truth now become form.

"We dull
our lives by
The WAY we
Conceive Them."

— James Hillman

goodbye self pity

❖ i stand alert at the door of my thoughts now.

❖ i say goodbye to self-pity thinking.

❖ i know i am not held to negative habits.

❖ FREEDOM OF SPIRIT is always mine.

❖ i give up feeling sorry and thinking sad thoughts.

❖ feeling sorry, even in small doses, is disempowering, i stop it.

❖ i am alert to my thinking
and feeling process. i direct thought.

❖ self-pity finds no expression today.
COURAGE REPLACES FEAR.

❖ old patterns of pity fall away now...possibility exists.

❖ no longer bound by regret or bitterness,
i act for what's next.

❖ i am THANKFUL for this new found freedom.

❖ self-concern is replaced
by concern for others. i serve people.

❖ i am grateful for good already received, as well as what's next.

❖ attention to GRATITUDE is an empowering attitude.

❖ gratitude opens door s to more good.

❖ self-pity opposes gratitude, today gratitude prevails.

❖ i reject self-pity.
i get engaged in life with others.

❖ Divine GOOD is always ever present...
it is my choice to notice it.

❖ today i notice the ALWAYS PRESENT GOOD NEWS.
i celebrate living with gratefulness.

❖ freedom of spirit is always mine.
i accept it today.
i accept plenty to spare and share.

i know when to hold and when to fold:

LIFE operates for, through and as me. There is one life, that life is God's life and that life is my life now. i live and move and have my being as this life. This life knows exactly what to do and how to do it to make TRUTH universally evident. Innovation is natural . i do whatever is called for in endless demonstrations, rehearsals, and as many starts and attempts as are required to bring forth what's new. i have courage. i have vitality. i am the evolution of will that's required.
i am the passionate expression
that easily takes on risk, without regret.
i RECOGNIZE MY STRENGTHS.
i compensate for any weakness.
i KNOW WHEN TO HOLD AND WHEN TO FOLD.

There is no resistance with me.
                no defenses stop me
                no opposition opposes me.
Innovation is natural to me, it is life and i accept,
the CREATIVE POWER of Infinite life, moving me forward.
i am exceedingly GRATEFUL.

i ACCEPT LIFE. I ACCEPT CHANGING
this word does it's work immediately,
i accept that right now. i am thankful that
i know when to hold and when to fold.
i am always guided going forward...
that's what's so. it is good.

self concern gives way...

Today, i include in my intention
all the people with whom i live and work
as well as all the people for whom i live and work.
All my complaints are turned into requests.
Today self-concern gives way to looking out for others.
Demands never exceed abilities.
as i prosper, all those around me are prospered also.

nothing is where everything comes from

God within and without, in us, as us, and with us,
Divine being, contributes
heart-powers of highest intentions for good, so that all of us
fulfill Divine destinies without wavering. we transcend all
illusion. As above, so below. we express the joy that is, as we
let go lack, limitation and suffering
to come into possession of what we seem to not have.

we go where now, we have nothing.
we are confident.
Nothing is, where everything comes from.....
This is the truth about us,
now and forever.
prospering happens.

about the flow of money...

❖ i deserve to be prosperous and wealthy.

❖ i deserve to be paid and receive money.

❖ i let money PASS THROUGH ME without worry.

❖ the MORE I GIVE, the more is given to me.

❖ i keep open about where i will receive money, i do not narrow
  my focus to certain people, places, situations or things.

❖ good comes FROM EVERYWHERE.

❖ i accept good with gratitude
  and willingness to prosper others, too..

❖ i freely receive good and give good.

❖ good is here and now. i look for it each day.
  i do not hold it on reserve for future moments.

❖ i have ALL the money i need and more to give.

❖ i give now,
  TRUSTING THE FLOW TO CONTINUE and it does.

❖ universe uncovers everything required. bye, bye worry.

❖ i feel friendly, loving and generous. fear is gone.

❖ my presence causes coincidences
  and happy surprises everywhere.

❖ CASH FLOWS THROUGH ME into the world,
  it returns to me increased and i keep on giving more...

❖ i always continue to keep up giving.

❖ it is okay to have everything and be happy.

❖ the world is a beautiful place of many generosities.

❖ i am a powerful being of light, my thoughts are bright.

❖ wealth contributes, i am radiant, sparkling and giving.

❖ i am financially successful. INCOME EXCEEDS EXPENSES.

❖ the more willing i am to prosper others,
  the more willing others are to prosper me.

❖ every dollar circulated comes back multiplied.

abundant thinking

❖ every day in every way things are getting better and better.
❖ i am a new, vibrant person. I AM GENEROUS.
❖ i have a sense of mastery over all the circumstances of my life.
❖ i am more than worthy of my many achievements.
❖ sufficiency has given way to Abundance.
❖ miracles occur naturally everywhere that i am.
❖ i attract money continuously. it is amazing.
❖ money forwards my action with ease.
❖ money is now so abundant, it doesn't need to be counted.
❖ MONEY COMES EASILY to me each day.
❖ i am on time, time works easily for me.
❖ good ideas come to me, prosperous ideas are put into action.
❖ i dare to prosper now and i do. i generate abundance.
❖ my wealth contributes to all those around me.
❖ more and more i see there is always plenty.
❖ i continue to participate with people
   who think in abundant ways.
❖ all that is PAST IS FREE TO LEAVE,
   i move ahead to what's next.
❖ all former fears have dissolved.
❖ enthusiasm and assurance increase each day.

more money affirmations

❖ money is getting more and more comfortable for me now...
❖ i feel free to spend...knowing there is always plenty.
❖ money is always on the way to me.
❖ i am letting go thoughts of scarcity. i have a good income.
❖ I NOW HAVE PLENTY OF MONEY.
❖ money is comfortable for me now, i share it freely.
❖ i know that the more i give, the more i get.
❖ I FREELY GIVE AND RECEIVE anywhere i am...
❖ my good comes from everywhere
   and anywhere and i accept it gladly.
❖ money flows into my life, new openings abound.
❖ cash flows through me into the world.
❖ ALL GIVING RETURNS TO ME MULTIPLIED.
❖ i continue to give
   no matter what is happening in my life
❖ it's easy to prosper others.
❖ income exceeds expenses, i am grateful. i prosper others.
❖ others are willing to prosper me, and i accept.
❖ my wealth contributes to the good of all people.
   finances are getting more and more abundant.
❖ new possibilities for money reveal themselves now.
❖ i look through all "appearances of limitation" knowing that
   prosperity will appear...i am assured.
❖ i let go of all poor ways of thinking and acting.
❖ i increase ideas of plenty today. i bless transactions.
❖ i do things which bring prosperity.
   i speak of money with confidence.
❖ i give without being asked. i am eager to give.

prosperity mind treatment

by Karen Lindsay

There is ONE LIFE, intelligence and love
in the universe, and that life is my life now.
THIS LIFE IS ABUNDANTLY GOOD.
Divine Mind guides, protects, and points out the way.

There is no limit to success in alignment with divine principle.
Fears and false ideas about success dissolve. Positive,
confident, clear thinking is now established. Highest levels of
creativity are manifested. Finances are abundant. False ideas
of lack and feelings of fear are now dissolved. Prosperity is
established now.
Supportive partnerships are formed and maintained.
Health and well being are constant.

Projects are completed quickly and easily. Each day's progress
is a source of satisfaction. i give thanks for being empowered
to do the work i love. i give thanks for the love
and support of family and friends.

I AM THANKFUL FOR DIVINE GUIDANCE.
This treatment is released and its good cannot fail...so it is.
This life is abundantly good. i am grateful.

i accept and i am willing

❖ i leave behind thoughts of not having enough.

❖ i leave behind resistance to having money.

❖ i leave behind resistance to generating money.

❖ i leave behind irresponsible attitudes about money.

❖ i leave behind excusing myself from doing
  what i want to do because of poverty.

❖ i leave behind manipulating others with a context of scarcity.

❖ i gladly accept responsibility that comes from abundance.

❖ i accept abundance as a place to express myself from.

❖ i accept expressing, i accept abundance
  and i express my true self.

❖ i am willing to use money
  to make the world work for everyone.

❖ i am willing to make life brighter
  and lighter for all those around me.

❖ i am willing to generate money
  to have the world work for everyone.

❖ i am willing to be conscious about money.

❖ i am willing to believe abundance is okay for me.

❖ i am willing to know money and to have money.,

❖ i am willing to handle what comes up about having money.

❖ i am willing to leave behind money as an imposition.

❖ i am willing to leave behind money as unnecessary.

❖ i do, what i really want to do, and have abundance.

❖ i am willing to be increasingly grateful
  as each new circumstance of prospering emerges.

❖ i am willing to teach others what i am learning.

❖ i am willing to handle plenty and excess
  so that prospering occurs wherever i am today.

i let go

❖ i drop feeling guilty about having money.
❖ i drop discomfort around spending money.
❖ i drop fear about the FLOW OF MONEY shutting down.
❖ i drop the idea that the poorer i am, the more spiritual i am.
❖ i drop "deserving" as an index of how much i allow myself.
❖ i DROP RESENTMENT of wealthy folks.
❖ i drop money, as a goal, in itself.

i am leaving behind

❖ i am leaving behind the ideas i learned about money.
❖ i am leaving behind the ideas
    I WAS TAUGHT ABOUT MONEY.
❖ i am leaving behind the ideas i accepted about money.
❖ i am leaving behind the ideas of money as a problem.
❖ i am leaving behind ideas of money as survival.
❖ i am leaving ideas of money as something i have to get...
❖ money is now a small link in the scheme of what i am about.

i see

❖ i see money as enabling me to make a difference.
❖ i see money as a way I GIVE TO MY WORLD.
❖ i see money as something to spread around.
❖ i see money is always around.
❖ i see money empowering me, to empower others.
❖ i see money as something to keep moving out with...
❖ I CAN GET MONEY ANYTIME.
❖ i see, i cause money to happen to me, by my thinking.
❖ i see money happens, by my expectation.
❖ i see everything, as an opportunity, to express money.

i know

❖ i can transform my relationship with money.
❖ i shift my way of seeing money,
and shift my life into service of others.
❖ i know i can not make much of a difference in the way the
world works, without using what the world works with...
❖ the unit or exchange in this world is money.
❖ i know i am willing to give up my hesitance about it.
❖ i know insufficiency of money
is due to thoughts of insufficiency.
❖ i know scarcity of money is due to thoughts of scarcity of $.
❖ i know money seeming hard-to-get
is due to thoughts of $ being hard to get.
❖ i know that if there is change in my money, that first there
will be A CHANGE IN MY THINKING about money...
❖ i know I AM READY for a change.

i realize

❖ i realize there is NO SCARCITY of anything in this world.
❖ i realize talk of scarcity exists
when ABUNDANCE IS APPARENT.
❖ i realize talk of scarcity comes from minds focusing on scarcity.
❖ i realize i CHOOSE MY FOCUS every moment.
❖ thoughts of scarcity cause scarcity.
❖ i realize thoughts of abundance cause and attract abundance.
❖ i realize all abundance starts in my mind first.
❖ i realize i am willing to think
in ways that will cause abundance.
❖ i realize i am willing to feel to cause abundance.
❖ i realize i am willing to "have" what i want.
❖ **i realize a great part of what i want is to serve others.**

i establish certitude of plenty

❖ there's plenty of business for everyone.

❖ goodbye to thoughts and feelings of lack and limitation.

❖ business comes from my opinions about business: today i have the opinion and attitude that there's plenty of business to spare, and even share; there's plenty where it all came from.
i'm assured of plenty.
i am certain of plenty.
i act for plenty
i establish certitude of plenty;
everywhere i am plenty is what's so.
everywhere i go plenty is what's so.
every time i speak plenty is what's so.
i am thankful, i show it,
i am thankful, i speak it,
i am thankful, i act it.

❖ everywhere i am, enrollment happens
everywhere i am, sales happen.
everywhere i am, upleveling of life happens.
i am grateful to be a source of courage, certitude and plenty for all those around me.

❖ i am a stand for life going forward to prosper and uplift all creatures in God's good plan for us all. that's what's so.

going forward

❖ today, i remember there is one Life...one Spirit...one Mind...
in which we live, move and have our being.
♥ we all manifest the life of INFINITE INTELLIGENCE.
♥ INFINITE INTELLIGENCE is never stopped
and neither am i.
♥ i am always going forward in greater wisdom.
♥ i am FREE OF ANY IDEA OF LACK or limitation,
no matter what the appearance.
all appearances are passing!
♥ all day today, i accept the invitation of life to go forward.
i create RICH NEW EXPERIENCES.
♥ i am living in an atmosphere of expansion.
♥ i have an attitude of blazing new trails.
♥ i expand on the good and prosper others as i go...
♥ all possibility and potentiality
exist today with me and through me.

always there is increase

- ❖ my good is here and now.
- ❖ i do not talk of beginning or end.
- ❖ I AM SATISFIED.
- ❖ always there is increase.
- ❖ i and this mystery here we stand.
- ❖ electrical increase now informs all my speaking silent and out loud.
- ❖ there is a perfect equanimity of all things.
- ❖ always there is increasing.
- ❖ God comes a loving bedfellow and sleeps at my side all night and leaves me baskets bulging with plenty. I AM SATISFIED.
- ❖ i have heard what the talkers were speaking. lack and limitation, beginnings and ends, but i do not talk of beginning or end.
- ❖ there was never more than there is now.
- ❖ there will never be any more perfection than there is now. Not any more heaven or hell than there is now.
- ❖ i celebrate myself and what i assume, you shall assume. i celebrate you. for every atom belonging to me as good, belongs to you.
- ❖ MY GOOD IS HERE AND NOW. so is yours. we do not talk of beginning or end.

An adaptation from LEAVES OF GRASS
– by Walt Whitman

waiter/waitress affirmations

❖ everyday is an opportunity to serve.
❖ each day people are happy with the way i serve them.
❖ GRATITUDE ABOUNDS wherever i am.
❖ gratuities abound wherever i am.
❖ people that i serve today are very generous.
❖ big tips come my way today.
❖ MY GRATITUDE PROSPERS ME.
❖ when i serve people i serve them fully.
❖ i am happy in my service of others.
❖ more money is circulated each day in tips.
❖ the more i serve others the more i am serving myself.

i am free to prosper in my business

The freedom of PERFECT PATTERN is my freedom now.
The creative power of my being is directed and expressed
excellently.
i am an excellent idea in the
    MIND OF INFINITE INTELLIGENCE.
Anything that seemed burdensome or boring is now
transformed by the renewal of my thinking. Left behind are
thoughts that suppress, scare or bind the life expression. i am
free to prosper in my business as an expression of life evolving.
What's possible is now occurring as outcomes.
        My business expresses my will-to-serve.
        i am happy to move forward serving my clients
                with good humor and pure joy.
        PROSPERITY is the continuing circumstance.
Expression of generosity, magnanimity and boundless potential
is everywhere that i am. i am an excellent idea directed and
expressed for the good of all.
i know what to do and i do it joyously producing results.
i am free to prosper in my business.
my business is blessed and prospered in all circumstances.
        PROSPERITY IS THE CONTINUING EVENT.
        Decisions are wise and capable.
        Goals are alive with vitality.
        i am the ability to prevail.
        THIS AWARENESS SETS ME FREE.
        i am grateful and blessed...
i give thanks that this word as cause is set in motion and does
not return void
...so it is. **i am free to prosper in my business.**

prosperity prevails

❖ what's required is always present.
❖ **prosperity prevails.**
❖ anytime i didn't have money, right after that, i got some.
❖ **prosperity prevails.**
❖ prosperity is well-being, is wealth, is assurance...
   all these are an inner conviction.
   i can have them when i feel them...
❖ **prosperity prevails.**
❖ plenty is a place, in mind, to be looking out from
      when i establish the idea of plenty in mind and
         feeling I SEE EVIDENCE OF PLENTY EVERYWHERE...
❖ **prosperity prevails.**
❖ prosperity is the perception
      of a process, on-going for ever,
      of such an abundance that it cannot be counted...
❖ **prosperity prevails.**
❖ today, i know, i am sure of this.
❖ **prosperity prevails.**

my giving makes me rich

❖ the more i give, the more i get...
❖ GIVING AND GETTING ARE THE SAME.
❖ the more i give...the more i get.
❖ today i leave behind thoughts of scarcity.
❖ money is for circulating today.
❖ generosity is a natural way of being.
❖ generosity improves my ability to remember that i deserve
  to prosper and so do you!
❖ i am willing today to give up hesitance about having
  and freely circulating money.
❖ i am transforming my relationship with money.
❖ my doubts about generosity are disappearing.
❖ giving is a natural extension of being.
❖ I ENJOY GENEROUS GIVING
  AND ABUNDANT RECEIVING.
❖ giving creates receptivity to getting.
❖ all that i give is multiplied and returned to me...
  universal eternal laws demonstrate time and time again.
❖ THE MORE I GIVE THE MORE i GET.
❖ i feel my natural urge to extend what i have...and today i act
  on it.
❖ i smooth the edges of any worries today by giving
  rather than by contracting and holding.
❖ i remember no one has ever become poor by giving.
❖ i give with a cheerful heart.
❖ the enthusiasm i have in giving, moves others to give more.
❖ i go beyond the thought that giving is a loss.
❖ i expand my ability to give generously.
❖ MY GIVING MAKES ME RICH.
❖ giving is an expression of trust in life.

increase through sharing

✤ today i let go all scarcity viewpoints.
  today i give rather than accumulate...
✤ I CHOOSE A PERCEPTION OF PLENTY.
✤ i look around to see what is wanted
  and needed so i can give more.
✤ i am pressing out... BEYOND what i thought my limits were...
✤ i am increasing my ability to respond generously
  and spontaneously in life daily.
✤ everything i have INCREASES THROUGH SHARING.
✤ i can always choose to share and give
  whatever i see as insufficient for me now... i do that.
✤ i am expanding my ability TO GIVE GENEROUSLY.
✤ today i am aware of the privilege it is to give and give freely.
♥ every day and every way things
  are getting better and better for everybody.
✤ the more i give, the more i get...
  GIVING MAKES ME RICH.

i give up scare-scarce thinking by giving

❖ i can only give what i have.

❖ i can only have what i am giving.

❖ great realizations are now taking place with me.

❖ true having is giving it all away.
   although this thought contradicts common thought, it's true.

❖ i can only
   GIVE WHAT I WOULD BE WILLING TO RECEIVE.

❖ i can only ever RECEIVE WHAT I'D BE WILLING TO GIVE.

❖ giving and having are the same.

❖ in order to receive i give first.

❖ i keep giving first.

❖ i give first,
   even when common thought makes it look dangerous.

❖ i give first...i understand
   and trust the workings of Universal Law.

❖ the preliminary step FIRST GIVING, ALWAYS GIVING
   vitalizes finances and causes great JOY.

❖ my perceptions are now reversed and turned right side up.

❖ i choose to give and relinquish scare-scarce thinking.

❖ i am liberated
   by my joyful always giving.

increasing income

❖ i live from intention rather than want...
❖ everything i circulate returns multiplied.
❖ everyday my income increases...
❖ everyday i am more and more grateful.
❖ THE MORE I GIVE, THE MORE I GET.
❖ my income increases miraculously.
❖ i have an abundant cash flow.
❖ whatever i circulate always returns.
❖ i replace all hesitant thoughts with action.
❖ on my income, there are no limits!
❖ my INCOME INCREASES EACH DAY in every way.

i tithe effortlessly and i prosper

❖ i give money easily.

❖ i am free to prosper.

❖ CIRCULATION replaces withholding in my life...

❖ i know the inner laws of success.

❖ as i tithe, so do i prosper.

❖ giving is the beginning of increase.

❖ i tithe easily, effortlessly, and consistently.

❖ i know the ancient universal laws are still true.

❖ I COUNT ON UNIVERSAL LAWS rather than appearances.

❖ the law of giving 10% of my income, prospers me today.

❖ i practice tithing and invoke the law in all my affairs.

❖ GIVING EFFORTLESSLY brings financial increase to me.

❖ my income reflects the grace of my giving.

❖ i share generously with organizations or people
 where i receive spiritual help.

❖ my faithful giving predicts beneficial outcomes for me.

❖ i voluntarily SHARE from my attitude of gratitude.

❖ i no longer believe i can "go broke" from giving.

❖ i no longer believe that withholding will make me successful.

❖ i no longer hold myself mentally in limitation.

❖ i faithfully give ten percent consistently.

❖ i invoke the power of increase by giving regularly.

❖ life is opening up to me now.

❖ I EXPECT THE BEST AND I GET IT.

❖ my good increases by circulating and sharing.

❖ i let go of little ways of thinking. i expand GREATER GIVING.

❖ greater giving insures greater receiving.

❖ my good comes quickly to me now.

generosity affirmations

- ❖ today i am EAGER to contribute.
- ❖ today i remember that the only way to receive is to give first...
- ❖ i don't wait to feel "comfortable" about giving, i give in the moment of now...
- ❖ i have a NEW WAY of being eager to contribute.
- ❖ instead of waiting to be asked, i offer...
- ❖ i represent a posture of easy giving CHEERFUL GIVING.
- ❖ giving is becoming more and more an important expression of who i am.
- ❖ giving produces a firm sense of esteem for me.
- ❖ the more i give the more I FEEL DESERVING of good for myself.
- ❖ esteem increases each time i give.
- ❖ the reciprocal action of giving and receiving makes everything in my life work well.
- ❖ the MORE I GIVE, the more i get...

increasing generosity

❖ today i am ever aware of the privilege
   it is to give, and give freely!
❖ i am looking around to see
   what is wanted and needed so I CAN GIVE MORE
❖ i see my natural urge to extend what i have... i act on it!
❖ i express myself by giving often and much i know what to do
   and i do it!
❖ i give away rather than accumulate and store up.
❖ more and more i am acknowledging and appreciating others!
❖ i am expanding my ability to give generously...
❖ i recognize that THINGS MULTIPLY when i let them go.
❖ all my giving is an investment in the future
   as well as an expression of my trust in life...
❖ my thinking is MORE WILLING about giving today.
❖ i enjoy generous giving and abundant receiving.
❖ all that i give is multiplied
   and returned to me, the more i give the more i get.
❖ giving is a grace.
   my DOUBTS about generosity ARE DISAPPEARING.
❖ generous giving is a way of being true to my highest ideals,
   systematic giving assures systematic receiving.
❖ the act of giving is freeing to my mind. i am grateful.
❖ i know EVERYTHING I HAVE INCREASES through sharing,
   so i share and give whatever i see as insufficient for me now.
❖ each day, i go beyond thought that giving is a loss!
❖ i have ability to GO BEYOND where stop with giving...
❖ giving creates my receptivity to getting.
❖ i am increasing ability to RESPOND GENEROUSLY,
   spontaneously, and intentionally.
❖ i know that no one has ever become poor by GIVING.

i create space for prospering

❖ i know that no one has ever become poor by giving.
❖ today i smooth edges of worry by GIVING,
   rather than by contraction and holding.
❖ my dependable giving, and generous attitudes & actions,
   outsmart my environment...so that many results appear.
❖ WHAT I AM GIVING is being given to me, increased...
❖ i give out of being, i give as a statement of my beingness...
❖ i give as an expression of the natural contribution that i am.
❖ my electrical enthusiasm
   around giving, moves others to join in giving...
❖ everyday in every way,
   things are getting BETTER AND BETTER for everybody!
❖ i extend myself infinitely
   by CONTINUING TO GIVE no matter what!
❖ ...today and tomorrow i press beyond
   what i thought my limits were yesterday...
❖ i let go all scarcity viewpoints today...
   i choose perceptions of plenty!
❖ i give with a CHEERFUL heart, my giving makes me rich!
❖ through my giving i establish
   A NEW, GENEROUS WAY of being.
   i am becoming more and more free in disbursements...
❖ It is through circulation
   that i create spaces and vacuums for new good to arrive .
❖ great generosity improves ability to be worthy of plenty!
❖ my present income
   is only the beginning
   of what is available,
   through giving freely
   my income increases daily.

the
ACORN
IS OBSESSIVE
it is ONLY AND ALL
CONCENTRATION,
UNDILUTED
LIKE A DROP
OF ESSENCE...
obsessively,
repetitively,
exhaustively...
the start of oak tree.

life is created with thought

❖ there is no reality in lack.
❖ no matter how distracting
  the appearance,
  abundance is everywhere present.
❖ my job is to set my mind and feelings
  IN ACCORD WITH ABUNDANCE
  that is always available.
❖ when i think in terms of plenty,
                abundance, prosperity, things changing...
                the picture improves
                as my thinking improves...
                right actions happen.
❖ IDEAS ARE UNDER OUTCOMES,
  they permeate and penetrate
  all appearances making them
  whatever i think they are...
❖ i am grateful to know my thought becomes result.
  all i require is already given...
  i open my thinking to all good.

mighty presence of God within

i am thankful to be heard
        extend to me the ability to comfort
        those in sorrow or in great need.

i am committed to MAKING A DIFFERENCE
because i am alive...
from the diamond shining mind of God,
wisdom and appropriate actions are intensified
for greatest best use...

i continue to SURRENDER MY WILL to God's will, as an
Ambassador of Divine love, and compassion.
radiance shines through my being. inspired i can know how to be,
        how to speak, how to act for the highest of good.

i am guided by the mighty presence of God within,
so that people are returned to remembrance
of power and presence.

my exercise of compassion is based on understanding
EVER PRESENT ETERNAL GOODNESS. Source of All Good,
always expressing loving care for creation
thankfully, DEPENDABLY.

it fills time and space...GOOD CAN NEVER END.
in all humanity i am able to see the beauty of DIVINE DESIGN.
Good HEALS SORROW and creates harmony again.
Gentle Presence heals discord and establishes joy.

i am willing to be contributed to...

"Those who believe in our ability...
create for us an atmosphere in which
it becomes easier to succeed."
                                        - J. L. Spaulding

✧ i accept help from others: i am still distinct as myself.
✧ i accept help from others: i don't claim to be
                               "better than" others.
✧ i accept help from others: they know i want things improved.
✧ i accept help from others: i am free to be helped.
✧ i accept help from others: they are welcome to KNOW ME.
✧ i accept help from others: i look at new information.
✧ i accept help from others: opportunities are stimulating.
✧ i accept help from others: obligation is not required.
✧ i accept help from others: it's okay to DEPEND ON OTHERS.
✧ i accept help from others: they are a contribution.
✧ instead of being devoted to doing things my own way
   i am now devoted to GETTING RESULTS.
✧ i make plenty of opportunities,
   to RECEIVE HELP and encouragement.
✧ when i have people helping me
   with my plans, I GET RESULTS.

prosperous provision has been made

❖ i talk about the good.
❖ today i banish limitation thinking.
          there is always plenty more of every good thing.
❖ i constantly acknowledge all the good that's here...
❖ unlimited good is mine today to share freely,
                    and i do share.
❖ sharing increases whatever i share...
❖ i demonstrate all kinds of good easily.
❖ goodness is uppermost in my mind today.
❖ i am loyal to thoughts of good today and tomorrow.
          Universal goodness is everywhere present.
❖ i accept good without question this week.
❖ i am constantly getting what i can accept.
❖ acceptance grows with me today.
❖ my thoughts adhere continuously to the idea of plenty.
❖ abundant provision has been made for me...
❖ prosperous provision has been made for me...
❖ i am successful in demonstrating plenty now.
❖ i give thanks often for all that i already have...
❖ visible supply of everything is seen by me today.
❖ my good vision is now certain to appear.

i trust that everybody prospers me

❖ i am GENEROUS and magnanimous.
❖ i am EAGER to prosper others
   and i do.
❖ others are happy and vitalized
   by prospering me.
❖ everyone prospers me...
   SUCCESS EXPANDS.
❖ i happily share
   increasing wealth.
❖ everybody helps me grow.
❖ my speaking
   has creative
   prospering power.

unceasing good

✤ people bring good unceasingly.
✤ i am always expressing generosity in new ways.
✤ The spiritual substance from which comes
   all visible wealth is never depleted.
✤ good comes from ALL THE PEOPLE around me.
✤ my assumptions about others
   create interactions and results.
   today i assume what i intend.
✤ PEOPLE RESPOND to my thinking about them
   by acting just like i say they will.
✤ my DEMANDS OF LIFE are expressed
   in my DAILY SPEAKING of life.
✤ in life i get what i want.
✤ WHAT I EXPECT shows up faithfully.
✤ i do not expect people to be or do what
            i have not been or done myself.
✤ i permit people to be the way they are.
✤ everyone represents an aspect of myself.
   people are my perceptions of them.
✤ today i have perceptions that prosper...
✤ each situation is an opportunity
   for prosperity to express.
✤ i think success. success outpictures in every way today.
✤ i expect "everybody prospers me".
✤ people count on me to prosper them and i do!!!
✤ GIVING AND GETTING are the same.

in an opulent universe

Today
- ❖ i graciously receive.
- ❖ i practice the art of receiving.
- ❖ i can have all that i can receive.
- ❖ i live in an opulent universe.
- ❖ there's PLENTY MORE where everything came from.
- ❖ receiving is an important aspect of opening up to life.
- ❖ i can have all that i will ACCEPT and use.
- ❖ i have all that i accepted already.
- ❖ the more i accept, the more i have to give.
- ❖ life is lived from within, outward.
- ❖ my ideas about receiving now ALLOW ME TO RECEIVE.
- ❖ the ideas that i hold as true create possibility for me.
- ❖ i feel worthy today.

change is the heart of my being

PERFECT PATTERN functioning at the level of consciousness is the source and cause of my success. The communication of the PERFECT PATTERN, the Universal Intelligence, with the particular is the eternal movement
and pattern shifting of evolution...
CHANGE IS THE HEART OF MY BEING.

i recognize my inherent expectation of good.
i am whole and free within the PERFECT PATTERN...
in fact PERFECT PATTERNS is what i am...
   i cut through negative feelings easily.
   i move quickly into postures and positions
   that bring good ever-increasing.
   i do not let any appearance stop me or thwart my intention.
CHANGE IS THE HEART OF MY BEING.

i am bold and free. i know my joyous expectations are fulfilled.
i give thanks that i expect to be the recipient
of many new opportunities for outcomes. i welcome each offer
to be, do and have more good. i align my thoughts with the
ONE MIND, the PERFECT PATTERN through all changes.
CHANGE IS THE HEART OF MY BEING AND i KNOW IT.
SUCCESS is the FORM, SHAPE and STRUCTURE of life now.
i KNOW MY EXPECTATIONS ARE FULFILLED.

i release these words of truth, they cannot return void...
these words do their work...
their work is already being done.

CHANGE IS THE HEART OF MY BEING...
and for this i give thanks.

prosperity teacher covenant

Money is a symbol of exchanging.
...avoiding relationship dissolves when people remember
money is simply a symbol of exchange - not an end in itself!
We are teaching the principles of true prospering for everyone.
Now, at the beginning of a new decade
    we dedicate ourselves to the unfoldment
    and full expression of a
    PROSPERITY COMMUNITY THAT IS GLOBAL.
We commit ourselves to the work
    of uncovering universal principles.
We live as the CONVICTION OF GIVING in all areas of life.
We understand giving ensures bountiful supply.
We live the practice of prosperity.
We realize the power of DIVINE PRINCIPLES.
We allow the DIVINE to work
    in and through thought, feeling, word and act.
We can be counted on to stand for
    the PRACTICE OF PROSPERITY.
We declare ourselves to be light
    that shines for the good of all.
DIVINE WILL abundantly provides us wisdom,
    love, well-being, equanimity, compassion and bountiful supply.
We make this covenant in trust, standing for
    prosperous exchange and real understanding
    in human beings as well as countries.
We surrender to the INNER FORCE OPERATING
    to bring us together
    in our shared work of teaching prosperity.

changing continues to bless me

God is all in all. GOD IS THE ONE LIFE,
ALL PRESENT, ALL KNOWING, ALL POWERFUL LIFE.
i live and move and have my being in this Life.
i receive ideas that point and aim me into changing.
i am an outlet for creative ideas.
changing moves things along...

i am enthusiastic and fully creative about changing,
even if i think otherwise.
CHANGING IS ALWAYS HAPPENING EVERYWHERE.
the law of Order is established.
great things are being accomplished.
       i am in motion for greater good.
       i let go of the negative.
       i let go of what is false.
       i let go of what limits me.
i am grateful. i am ready to let go of old good...
new good occurs.
right action is now happening.
relinquishment prevails, harmony prevails.
i am fully creative about changing. good responds.
i use it with full authority and CONFIDENCE in all aspects of
my business, projects and relationships. i speak, think and feel
what i intend. my words, inner conversations,
outer speaking, and feelings are congruent good.

EVERYDAY BRINGS GREATER GOOD:
new ideas, more revelations,
and increased blessings for all.
i am renewed by the power of this word.
i am grateful.
i release this word to the law of perfect outworking.
Changing continues to bless me.

declaration for prosperity teachers

We declare that we come together to take
on the enlightening practice
of TEACHING PROSPERITY PRINCIPLES
with compassion and clarity.

Today we surrender to
THE INNER FORCE
which is operating to bring us together
in our shared work

With Heavenly Strength, Universal Commitment
and a Radical Understanding OF INCREDIBLE LOVE ...
We come together to Serve a high purpose.
We answer the call of Service. In being awake to who we are
there is only Service ...The Divine moves us to reveal
the prosperous awakening truth in all beings.
Serving moves life. The ones we serve continue to serve others,
everything works together for good.
Everyone is discovering authorship of circumstance.

We guide beings in ways according to their mentalities.
We appear in the midst of many activities
without ever leaving the presence of Divine Intuition.
We proceed instructed by great spiritual benefactors...
with tireless will, we build up roots of goodness...
with unbroken commitment and continuity we carry out
practices of enlightening beings everywhere.
We work using generosity and magnanimity.
We work with compassionate speech and beneficial actions.

We uncover remembrance of UNIVERSAL PRINCIPLES
in everyone.
We are imbued with light. We are happy in our work together.
We provide a clearing so people can give up fears... they give up
limitation... they let go self concern... they see themselves in
others... they are sharing, revealing, and exchanging.
Our teaching subtracts fear. Our teaching adds nothing,
and NOTHING IS WHERE EVERYTHING COMES FROM.

We teach the true nature of coming and going.
Actions and teaching spontaneously arise in perfect timing.
We benefit all living beings. We are always prosperity teachers.

We look upon the world with active great compassion. We know
everything as an extension (perfectly mirroring)...what we are.
That we are PROSPERITY TEACHERS, is a fine self-
appointment. Imbued with light, empowered by shared
commitments, we are guided in dispelling miseries of worlds.
Our work is directed and blessed...the way is ever always,
already revealed in the moment.
We embody enlightenment for the good of all,
            as we continue to surrender
            to the INNER FORCE which is
            operating to bring us together
            in our shared work
            as prosperity teachers.

teaching prosperity in the company of others

in conformity with the dedication
practiced by enlightening beings of all times

 my life shows up in the way of magnanimous heart
 freeing all hearts from suffering. i am grateful.
 i do not seek the unexcelled way for my own sake...
 my purpose is TO ENABLE
 all sentient beings to attain liberation
 from lack, limitation, and scarce possibility.

each day I BECOME MORE DETERMINED.
   i do not give up or run away.
   i am not shocked or frightened.
   i am not discouraged or intimidated.
   i am not made tired by the effort.
   i continue to be determined to enable others.

those who are revolving in repeated routines according to the force of their acts and erroneous views. i enable them. Those in cages of suffering the web of attachments to desires or acting like crazy victim, all are awakening to powerful perceptions. i enable them as i am enabled. i cultivate enlightening practices in all my work. i am grateful to be joined with a past present future continuum of others just like me.

> we carry out our shared work happily.
> we practice generosity quite gladly.
> we are leaders.
> enabling others as we are enabled.

showing the way to safety and peace, we serve and provide for others using appropriate means to inform them of truth and possibility.
in our company, people prosper.
good company is established. error is annihilated.
wrongdoing is cleared away, roots of goodness are discovered.
people are freed from doubt.
WE ARE TEACHERS OF PROSPEROUS WAYS.

like the sun, we shine universally without seeking thanks. we diligently practice dedication to the prosperity of all beings with joyful hearts. We develop hearts of great compassion in this way. we give thanks for lives that continuously serve others.

i am a prosperity teacher

❖ GOD is all in all...
DIVINE INTELLIGENCE always moves forward.
❖ So do i...never apart from Divine Intelligence...i am changing.
❖ SOMETHING WONDERFUL IS HAPPENING...i am ready.
❖ i see perfection behind all appearances of limitation.
❖ i am guided by my true nature to express truth...
i AM A PROSPERITY TEACHER.
❖ achieving prosperity easily...i reflect good by thinking good.
❖ i waste no energy on fear or doubt... i go forward now.
❖ No seeming of lack or limitation disturbs me.
❖ i am not deterred by delay or false appearances.
Detours do not confuse me.
❖ i remember PLENTY IS ALREADY ALWAYS
the circumstance.
❖ i see truth in all appearances now.
❖ i win seeming financial games of life easily,
faithfully and for everyone's benefit.
❖ When i win EVERYONE AROUND ME prospers.
❖ Teaching prosperity is easy for me.
❖ i remember i am only ever teaching myself.
❖ i teach best what i most need to learn.
Whatever i teach i learn. i am thankful.
❖ Divine Mind is an ever reliable source of supply,
available for constant use. i am grateful.
❖ i have immediate access to all that's intended.
❖ in a world of plenty, i have plenty to spare and share.
❖ i see the best in everything. gratitude prevails with me.
❖ i know the truth of being, life is blessed wherever i am.

"all forms
Of AUTHENTIC
EXISTENCE
spring from
VISION and are
a VISION... all that
springs from VISION
exists to produce
IDEAL FORM..."

— Plotinus III·8·7

i choose changing

"many are called, few choose."

– anonymous

*"faith does not change conditions,
it changes the way we relate to them."*

– anonymous

❖ CHANGING is okay with me today.
❖ being convinced of the VALUE IN CHANGING,
   i choose it.
❖ this is a perfect, appropriate day for changes.
❖ i am willing for change.
   i am thankful for process.
   i give up waiting for a more perfect
   time to make chosen changes.

❖ CHANGING BLESSES me and the people around me.
❖ the creating power of mind is put to use
   for subtle, quick, beneficial changes.
❖ today I INVITE CONTRIBUTION.
   i am willing to be and have more.
   i let go stuck opinion.
   i see stunning examples of plenty.

❖ i BREAK UP what's no longer productive.
❖ today i choose changing.

i am associating with people who empower me

❖ i am willing to DEMONSTRATE ABUNDANT LIFE.
❖ i am willing to be encouraged and inspired to action...
... to be moved in the direction i was headed.
... to associate with people who empower me.
❖ i overcome unproductive work patterns.
i deserve encouragement that is purposeful and committed.
I RISE ABOVE RESTRICTION. i accept help.
i am receptive to suggestions.
❖ i plan to be with others in new ways so that we forward the action in each others' lives.
❖ i surrender to a process of being coached,
i share winning with those who coach me.
❖ i am willing to invite and REQUEST RIGOROUS SUPPORT from my allies and also, to give it.
❖ I ADMIT WHAT I DON'T KNOW and request help.
❖ i am receptive to input that forwards progress.
❖ i make necessary requests to start, work on, and complete jobs.
❖ i develop new listening for prompting projects.
i share new ideas.
❖ i answer questions about goals so others can support me.
❖ i am accountable for unfinished work.
❖ I MAKE PROMISES for tasks and deadlines.
❖ i project ideas and attract support that produces results.
❖ ideas are no longer exclusive property, i share them freely.
❖ i am supportable, willing to refine ideas with others.
❖ i brainstorm on projects with others.
❖ i acknowledge and GIVE THANKS for support attracted.
❖ i am enlivened by support.

i work successfully
with others helping me

*"nothing can be itself without being
in communication with everything else"*
                              - Thomas Berry

❖ terrific ideas GO SOMEWHERE with me.
❖ in order to get things done, i get lots of help.
❖ i have powerful partners and active associations.
❖ MENTORS and COACHES help me to win in working.
❖ i allow support to make a difference.
❖ conversations of hesitation no longer direct me.
❖ i have WINNING CONVERSATIONS that keep me
   committed to accountability, for results.
❖ i am open to the help i am requesting. i let it in.
❖ dreams of motion now become REAL ACTIONS.
❖ ACCOMPLISHMENTS MULTIPLY
   with contribution from others.
❖ i am grateful to have help required
   to OVERCOME UNPRODUCTIVE WORK PATTERNS.
❖ widespread response comes from habitual reaching out
❖ i spend more and more time with people
   who are committed to getting things done.

blessing all people

❖ i call blessing forth, for all people.
❖ i LET GO mistaken views of people today.
❖ every person has real worth and value...
to remember this, has a moderating influence on how i see.
❖ all people have intelligence and goodness innate in them.
❖ i practice COMPASSION in my regard for others today.
❖ each individual is important and precious to life...
❖ today i have an accurate view of people.
❖ i give up the idea that anyone is bothersome or unimportant.
❖ i OPEN MY EYES TO SEE who people really are today.
❖ i relate to people from a new perspective now.
❖ i notice how people express

life
order
intelligence
perseverance
and joy.

❖ individuals respond to being found precious.
❖ there is a continual process of OPENING UP
to see people in a new, wonderful way.
❖ The more i love, the MORE I PROSPER...

i express praise easily

✤ i proclaim the good.

✤ i speak Divinely...my vocabulary is life-giving.

✤ i EXPRESS PRAISE EASILY... my speaking is constructive.

✤ acknowledging others is a usual activity for me.

✤ i understand that what i praise increases.

✤ whatever is good for me i APPRECIATE with spoken words.

✤ my WORDS OF PRAISE are powerful and loving.

✤ appreciation expressed daily lightens up life for everyone.

✤ RICH IDEAS OF GOOD are ever present in my language.

✤ the Mind and Heart of Being respond favorably to PRAISE.

✤ OPPORTUNITIES INCREASE for acknowledgment each day.

✤ i give up gossip and undermining conversations.

✤ whatever i give RETURNS MULTIPLIED to me.

✤ thanksgiving is becoming a WAY OF LIFE for me.

✤ the POTENT POWER OF PRAISING is always used by me.

✤ there is a UNIFYING UPLIFTING POWER
   in all praising everywhere.

✤ i like what my words produce...i speak affirmatively.

✤ the tone of my voice expresses GREAT APPRECIATION.

✤ my SPEAKING creates expanding good for everyone.

✤ my consciousness has attracting power.

✤ the WORDS OF MY MOUTH are purposeful and inspired.

✤ i praise, rejoice and express easily today.

✤ i express PRAISE everyday.

creativity

"You are merely the lens in the beam. You can only receive, give and possess the light as the lens does. If you seek "your rights" you prevent the oil
>>> *and air from meeting*
>>> *in the flame*
>>> *you rob the lens*
>>> *of its transparency,*
your capacity, that is, to vanish as an end, and remain purely as a means" — *Dag Hammarskjold*

things appear at the command of thinking

There is no restriction to good in creative presence.
Mighty Intelligence is always everywhere at work...
i am one with Intelligence. i am never apart from what i am.
MIND OF GOD is operating, through me, at the level of
acceptance. i am surrounded by POSSIBILITY.

i am not in bondage to limitation or lack. Barriers in my
thinking are all that hold me in any position... Since there are
no real barriers in thinking, there are no real barriers in any
position. i realize this liberating truth today.
I AM FREE TO PROSPER.

PROSPERITY IS IDEAS OF LIMITLESSNESS.
Things come and go but the idea of plenty endures.
Things appear at the command of thinking and assumption.
Today i accept ideas of plenty, as my ideas.
i know IDEAS ARE SOURCE OF OUTCOMES.
i give thanks for every evidence of financial improvement.
i am confident that Divine resource never fails.
These words go forward and do their work,
their good cannot fail...
Things appear at the command of my thinking.

i speak prosperous results

"Nothing is contrary to the laws of nature,
only what we know about the laws of nature."
- *St. Thomas Aquinas*

❖ whatever i speak is what i am creating...
❖ i SPEAK PROSPEROUSLY. i am a clear thinker.
❖ i am on the road of already abundant life....
❖ in specific terms of supply and support, I TALK PROSPERITY...
   my emotions resonate with true prospering.
❖ i affirm the GOOD I INTEND.
❖ i speak success in the very face of question...
   MY WORDS RESONATE WITH TRUE PROSPERING.
❖ i speak success in the face of all doubt.
❖ results are attained by my speaking...
   i have a PROSPERING CONSCIOUSNESS.
❖ i am accomplished in DEMONSTRATING PLENTY
   of what i intend.
❖ i SEE OPPORTUNITIES rather than obstacles.
❖ i take direct actions. i move to what's intended.
❖ the quality of life improves,
   for everyone, whenever i am present.
❖ at night, MY LAST THOUGHTS ARE OF GOOD...

making new choices

"God is all in all
God is the One Life, all present ...all knowing ...all powerful life.
WE LIVE AND MOVE AND HAVE OUR BEING
IN THIS ONE LIFE.
We are the point where life causes form thru thought.
Now, old patterns have given way to
REFRESHING NEW ONES.
We are enthusiastic and aglow.
Our prayers have been answered...
    We have accepted the answers.
    New alternatives are unfolding.
    We are MAKING NEW CHOICES.
We no longer settle for less than what's appropriate.
We have left behind everything and everybody ... that does not
serve a Divine plan for us.
    EVERYTHING MOVES FORWARD.
    We let the good come in.
    We welcome the leading of great good.
Receptive hearts and minds love possibility.
We enjoy a PATH OF PLENTY ...
a path of increasing good.
        Divine Intelligence has cleared the passage ...
constant revelation happens, INCOME INCREASES ...
self changing is successful. We give thanks.
Love is enriching our nature ... magnifying, purifying
            and elevating our nature.
        Always there is good increase.
        Our intuition is one with light.
Our world is ALIVE WITH DIVINE PROSPERING ...
        everyday brings greater good.
This word now goes forth to outpicture, as manifestation.
            And, so it is.

new year mind treatment

...for this new year, these words will produce the desired result, they are operated on by a POWER greater than i am as a singular self. Good alone goes from me. Good alone returns to me. There is One LIFE, DIVINE, perfect and ever flowing. i am grateful that i am a manifestation of living SPIRIT...
 i give thanks to be created and maintained by
 that ONE PRESENCE
 that ONE POWER
 that ONE DIVINE PATTERN
This year there is perfect assimilation and perfect elimination.
 There is NO CONGESTION... NO CONFUSION...
 NO INACTION... NO FEAR...
 NO DOUBT... NO HOLDING BACK.
 i am letting that PERFECT DIVINE PATTERN flow.
 i take action appropriate to intentions.
 i have appropriate repose between actions.
i let go resignation and stagnation. i reclaim the passion and peacefulness that works perfectly. in full freedom, i work effectively to make dreams come true for all people around me, too. the conversations i create have powerful partnership networking, everyone wins ... speaking creates ever MORE POSSIBILITY for true goals and real love... i reclaim and walk the line destined for me by most high expression of the ONE PRESENCE AND ONE POWER... my will is surrendered to the will of highest expression. i produce trust and love with conversations.
This year i am commitment in action. i overcome all seeming difficulty. Whatever is mine comes to me. The DIVINE guides all actions... i make up intentions about many outcomes. What's next is always PERFECTLY OUTPICTURING.
i give thanks. This word, as cause, is set in action and cannot return void... and so it is.
i am grateful beyond measure, now today.

expectancy treatment

*"The disharmony of the unwise
is confounded by God's ever present wisdom."* – *anonymous*

*"For I hold what God wills above what I will. I cleave to God as
servant and follower; my impulses are one with God's, my pursuit is
one with God's; in a word my will is one with God's"* – *Epictetus*

Everything necessary to success is already established...
Already with me...TODAY i AM ALREADY EXPECTING GOOD.
i am expecting good success in all actions...
        each thing that i do,
        each task that i complete,
        each activity that i am in,
        is created and fulfilled.
All that i do represents initiative, wisdom, love.
i rejoice in all life is doing everywhere. Process progresses.
i am guided to appropriate thoughts, feelings and actions.
Life succeeds in and through projects and endeavors.
Everything necessary to success is already established...
Already everything necessary is being brought to fruition...
satisfaction is present. Nothing delays GOD'S GOOD IDEAS
from manifestation.
i creatively direct, select, choose, move into actions...
unfoldment of good takes place . i am creative,
Intelligence is ACTIVE in my affairs and in all people...
i experience JOYOUS COOPERATION.
i prosper others and i am prospered.
ABUNDANCE OF LIFE is available today.
i accept it manifesting in and through me.
I AM GRATEFUL. what was behind me in all past success, is
behind me now. i expect GOOD PROSPEROUS RESULTS. i
expect to share my prospering.
This word, as cause, is set in action. So it is.

good is certain

i recognize One Power in the Universe,
ONE PERFECT PATTERN... One Intelligence, only One.
i am part of Intelligence which is overseeing all action,
all reaction, all reforming, developing and completion.
i am WITH and IN the creative impulse
which forms worlds as well as situations,
events and circumstances...

Today whatever bothers, frustrates, pains, or angers
is a powerless idea without my power of acceptance.
i CLEAR MIND and thinking of all old reactive habits.
i am glad this is so. It has a softening effect.

My emotional commitment today is to good.
    i EXPECT GOOD AND i GET IT.
    i responsibly act for good and promote confidence.
    i direct attention to good.
    i direct imagination to the perfection
    and FULFILLMENT OF GOOD INTENTIONS.
    i dismiss all appearances of conflict.
    i move through apparent defeat to renewed confidence.
    The power to wait patiently is active with me.
    i inhere in clear action and purpose.
    i move into appropriate actions in timely ways.
    MY GOOD IS CERTAIN. i am grateful.

i TRUST THAT GOOD IS ALREADY ALWAYS CERTAIN,
NOT ONLY POSSIBLE, BUT CERTAIN. i give thanks.
these words work...
Even as i speak they are already accomplished in time and space.
They do not return void... GOOD IS CERTAIN.

good is assured

God is all in all. GOOD IS NATURAL. i am part of all that is...
INTELLIGENCE and my mind are the same;
ONE EVOLVING SYSTEM.

Thoughts project ideas into form. i give up harrowing thoughts
that anything is lacking in anyone, anything, or any
circumstance. whenever it seems something is missing, i go to
work on thought, first off ... immediately.
THERE IS ALWAYS PLENTY
OF WHATEVER IS REQUIRED...

good as infinite supply is present now and always.
i relax in remembering this...
i speak the word to create appropriate outcomes...
THERE IS SUCCESS and a feeling of freedom present.

Now there is elimination to any psychological pattern seeming
to limit experiences of unending supply and true good. i wipe
out any belief in lack that limits good. i change outlook and
scarcity perceptions.
i ACCEPT ONLY IDEAS OF GOOD.

This word is now established in being.
i give great thanks that this is so.
i release concern by knowing GOOD IS ASSURED.

declaration of Divine order

i declare that God is all there is...one power, one presence,
active ever always. There is nothing opposed to God.
Divine order is ever present,
ever active as on-going creation:
> forming
> developing
> making
> breaking and
> reforming

People embrace the human race.
As galactic beings, we are open and receptive to a universe of
good possibility ... to Divine ideas of RESOLUTION and peace
...to evermore CHALLENGES OVERCOME ...to expression of
good fortune for all ...to expanded hope and freedom and
alliances for FURTHER EVOLUTION.

DIVINE PATTERN permeates and transcends this world.
Everything moves according to this Intelligence.
We are living in a SPIRITUAL UNIVERSE NOW...
Its government is INTELLIGENCE...
Its laws are INTELLIGENCE, acting as laws.

One power, one presence is always ever...
> ONLY active.
> That's what's so.

renunciation decree

i promise to give up attachment to:
    anxieties
    sorrow
    depression
    confusion
    obstruction
    all hardships
    bondage of any kind
    all feelings of anger
    dangling ropes of doubt
    miserable conditions and
    the obstacle of inappropriate companions
i declare that:
    threats
    delusions
    meannesses
    fears of calamity
    the perils of life
    inappropriate acts
    wrong means of livelihood
    false discrimination
    and mundane routines
no longer have any power over me.
Clinging to what is not well-intended is now
                dissolved and given up.
                    - adapted from Avataka Sutra

"prosperity
is not in the
possession of things
but in the
recognition
OF SUPPLY
and in the knowledge
OF FREE... ACCESS
to an inexhaustible
storehouse of all
that is GOOD
or DESIRABLE."

-CHARLES FILLMORE (1936)

About the author

Toni Stone,
is a New England writer and quilter,
teaching the metaphysical and ethical
SKILLS OF PROSPERING
to entrepreneurs.

Working out of the home base of New Thought,
for over three decades, her key message:
GIVING BEGINS EVERYTHING
has made her a well-loved, appreciated CONSULTANT
to business owners all over the country.

The author has great experience, intuition
and first hand information to share about putting pieces together
so that PROSPERING OCCURS IN EVERY SEASON.

She assists people discovering and being accountable for
their own PROSPERITY POSSIBILITY.
She says PROSPERING IS AN INSIDE JOB.

She lives in Vermont with her husband
and has a clear view of the Green Mountains.

For information about classes and consulting
Call (802) 849-2257
or on the web at www.wonderworks.org.

Order Form

	Price Each	Quantity	Total Price

Toni Stone's Prosperity Affirmations
From the original **Seasons of Prosperity...** affirmations for financial increase
and appropriate wide seeing attitudes that have been used successfully.
These sets are for writing and repeating each day. Good for beginners.
60 pages plus glossy, full color cover ....$9.99 _____ _____

Seasons of Prosperity–SPRING Affirmations and Intentions
Affirmation for the Spring Cycle and beginnings.
138 pages plus glossy, full color cover ....$24.99 _____ _____

Seasons of Prosperity–SUMMER Affirmations and Intentions
Affirmation for the Summer Cycle and working hard.
98 pages plus glossy, full color cover .... $24.99 _____ _____

Seasons of Prosperity–AUTUMN Affirmations and Intentions
Affirmation for the Autumn cycle and endings.
138 pages plus glossy, full color cover .... $24.99 _____ _____

Seasons of Prosperity–WINTER Affirmations and Intentions
Affirmation for the Winter cycle and resting.
138 pages plus glossy, full color cover ....$24.99 _____ _____

DELIBERATE DESIGN–Affirmations for Every Kind of Day
ADVANCED AFFIRMATIONS for everyday use. Includes 12 qualities affirmations
for cycles. Peace declaration from the early 1900's and many future oriented treatments.
72 pages plus glossy, color cover ....$9.99 _____ _____

SAFETY PREVAILS–Affirmations for Dissolving Discords
Thoughts for attitude adjustments in times of stress, inner and outer.
Weather, chaos, difficulties and dissensions.
108 pages plus glossy, color cover ....$15.99 _____ _____

TONIC FOR THE MIND–Affirmations for Improved Relationships
Mind Treatments for getting along, letting go and being satisfied. Also includes
intentions for healing and those who have died as well as those people who require
prospering...pages to write names for each.
134 pages plus glossy, full color cover ....$15.99 _____ _____

Full Leather SEASONS OF PROPERTY: Classic Edition
Four season affirmations, treatments and intentions for the earth. Includes how to
write a mind treatment, as well as the qualities each season, derived from American Indian lore.
300 pages plus FULL LEATHER cover .... $75.00 _____ _____

Prosperity Practitioners's Handbook: Pocket Size Edition: Re-issue
The original 1986 collection of affirmations for prosperous results, health, forgiveness,
partnership, peace, progress, and overcoming chaos...includes prosperity teacher covenant.
74 pages plus full color cover ....$9.99 _____ _____

IS MONEY THE MATTER? Chapter Three: The Prosperity Principles
A BEGINNERS MUST for the 27 Principles of Prospering with valuable distinctions about
behavior changes required for prospering...points out patterns in thinking as well as
invisible attitudes that must shift to prosper...An exacting series of essays that have been
used to coach and teach thousands of people in the past 30 years.
146 pages plus glossy, full color cover ....$15.99 _____ _____

IS MONEY THE MATTER? Chapter Eight: Tools to use for Prospering.
Tools, Tasks and Plans for a Successful Prosperity Practice. Full instructions for image
books, self talk tapes, context tithing and other prosperity practices that have been
proven workable for thirty years.
166 pages plus glossy, full color cover ....$15.99 _____ _____

Toni Stone's Guide to Prosperity... Nine Year Cycles
Assessment of each year in The Nine Year Cycle. directions for finding yours...
checking past patterns...knowing what appropriate timing is.
32 pages plus glossy, full color cover ....$15.00 _____ _____

Daybook & Prosperity Journal (Available for Winter, Spring, Summer or Autumn)
A 13 week Journal featuring quotes, things to do, calls to make, affirmation space
to write, plus a full page daily schedule. Inspiring cover photos by Marie Pappas.
Some Toni Stone Quilt pictures also. Fits week at a glance covers.
186 pages plus glossy, full page cover ....$24.99 _____ _____

The Naked Loon
Random essays on living a complete, conscious life as a prosperity practitioner
in today's world.
60 pages plus glossy, full page cover..$9.99 _____ _____

	Price Each	Quantity	Total Pri

More Than A Pinecone
Short pieces about harvesting rich wisdom from everyday seedy aggravations... helpful to keep a prosperity perspective.
64 pages plus glossy, full page cover .... $15.99 _____ _____

Grateful Holiday Season
Celebrating affirmations, Quotes, prayers, and even vegetarian meat-like recipes from training weekends in winter. Good reminders for the Holiday Spirit. Good gift book for affirmative minded friends.
44 pages plus glossy, full color cover .... $9.99 _____ _____

A Prosperous Thought for the Day
A light-hearted oracle of one minute prosperity advice used by Toni for wake up calls in Boston and New York in the late eighties when a computer called her students each morning at their request to keep them on the beam and prospering. Pick a number one to sixty-four for your day's wisdom. Pieces can be used for answering service, as well.
72 pages plus glossy, full color cover. .... $9.99 _____ _____

Extreme Prospering...Tithing and How it can be done...
A short engaging text about the how's & why's of tithing which includes various people's experience of tithing too.
64 pages plus glossy, full color cover. .... $9.99 _____ _____

Toni Stone's Cold Season Cookbook
Recipes and food lore for the holidays and bringing you through the quiet season.
56 pages plus glossy, full color cover. .... $9.99 _____ _____

Toni Stone's Writing Practice Journal
With Affirmations and Blank pages for journaling .... $9.95 _____ _____

What I Say is What I Am
An affirmation collection of self talk.
68 pages plus glossy, full color cover. .... $12.60 _____ _____

What I Say is What I am... Part Two
Affirmations, delcarations, mind treatments and prayers for the next decade.
68 pages plus glossy, full color cover. .... $12.60 _____ _____

Study Books for Every Season
Seasonal collections of quotes, affirmations and intentions. Plus fill-in pages for gratitude and goals as well as healing treatment and those who have gone before treatment with pages ..to list the names of the intended person. Included are Zodiac overviews of sun sign characteristics to be called forth as well as tendencies to be dissolved with listing pages for Zodiac goals to be completed. Small, compact books with lay-flat, spiral binding for easy access on phone calls. Some also have extra pages for daily promises.
56 to 62 pages plus glossy, full color cover .... $12.50 each _____ _____

Spring–What's Required is Always Present ....Purple crocus cover with lavender pages _____ _____
Spring–No Limits Allowed No Limits Exist ....Pink Tulip cover with bright pink pages _____ _____
Spring–Ready for Confident Changing ....Flower cover with light pink pages _____ _____
Summer–Change is Required ....Yellow gerber daisy cover with yellow pages _____ _____
Summer–We Have What It Takes ....Sunflower cover with bright gold pages _____ _____
Autumn–Giving Begins Everything ....Orange Leaves cover with kraft brown pages _____ _____
Autumn–Finding Harvest in its Season ....Myriad squash cover with bright orange pages _____ _____
Winter–Dissolving Legacies of Limitation ....Snowy backyard cover with sky blue pages _____ _____
Winter–Standing Firm in Expectation ....Pinecone cover with dusty sand pages _____ _____
Winter–Gratefully Gathering in Winter ....Snowy woods cover with light blue pages _____ _____

Send Your Order to:

Wonder Works Studio
401 Buck Hollow Road, Fairfax, VT 05454
(802) 849-2257 • fax 802-849-6552 • www.wonderworks.org

Name: _____

Address: _____

City: _____ State: ____ Zip: _____

Phone: _____

e-mail:_____
If you would like to receive random essays from Toni Stone

Sub-total: $ _____

Priority shipping & handling
$3.00 x book = $ _____

TOTAL: $ _____